INSIDE THE
WHALE
AND OTHER ANIMALS

INSIDE THE
WHALE
AND OTHER ANIMALS

Illustrated by Ted Dewan
Written by Steve Parker

A Doubleday Book for Young Readers

DK

A Dorling Kindersley Book

Project Editors *Scott Steedman*
Mina Patria
Art Editor *Nigel Hazle*
Production *Norina Bremner*
Managing Editor *Simon Adams*
Managing Art Editor *Peter Bailey*

A Doubleday Book
for Young Readers

Published by Delacorte Press
Bantam Doubleday Dell Publishing
Group, Inc.
666 Fifth Avenue
New York, New York 10103

This work was first published in
Great Britain in 1992 by
Dorling Kindersley Limited
9 Henrietta Street
London WC2E 8PS

Library of Congress
Cataloging in Publication
Data will appear in
subsequent editions.

ISBN 0-385-30651-2

Color reproduction by
Dot Gradations, Essex, England

Printed in Belgium by Proost

TO MÉMÉ

NO ANIMALS WERE CUT UP OR
EVEN EMBARRASSED IN THE
PREPARATION OF THIS BOOK

CONTENTS

INTRODUCTION

As a curious and intelligent person, you probably wonder what goes on inside things. Maybe you've even taken apart a broken radio or an old watch, just to see what makes them tick. Animals are the ultimate machines, but looking inside one on the kitchen table could be a bit trickier– especially if that animal is a whale.

Each of our twenty-one animals is in some way special. Why no familiar creatures such as cats, dogs, and horses? Because they're all mammals, and their insides are fairly similar. We wanted to poke around in the corners of the animal kingdom, among the frogs and snails and spiders, to explore their fascinating, intricate, and, often beautiful anatomy.

All animals do the same basic things: breathe, eat, digest, get rid of wastes, sense the world, move about, and reproduce. But like vehicles on a roadway, from an electric minicar to a giant diesel truck, each has something different under the hood. The rattlesnake can wrap its jaws around a victim bigger than its head, the bee has five hearts, and the octopus's throat goes through the middle of its brain. The starfish doesn't even have a brain, but it can spill its stomach out of its mouth. Each has come up with a very different design solution to the age-old problems of living.

For in nature, there's more than one way to skin a cat.

Ted Dewan

Steve Parker

BLUE WHALE

BIGGER THAN ANY DINOSAUR, the blue whale is the largest creature ever to live on earth. By the time it becomes a teenager it is 100 feet long and weighs more than 30 elephants. Yet when the whale opens its gigantic mouth, it is usually to swallow shrimplike creatures called krill, each one the size of your finger. In summer, the blue whale eats four tons of krill – about four million of them – every day. In winter, when krill are scarce, it survives mainly on its own body fat.

As it roams the world's oceans, the whale must come to the surface every few minutes. For it is not a fish but a mammal, and like all mammals it breathes air.

BLOWHOLE
This is the whale's nostril or breathing hole. Water pressure closes it on diving, but some water still trickles in. On surfacing, the whale blows this, and vapor from its lungs, into the sky in a fountain 32 feet high.

LUNGS
In proportion to body size, a whale's lungs are smaller than a human's. But it changes nine tenths of the air in them with each breath, whereas people change only one eighth.

Muscle

Brain

Nasal passage

Skull

Skull bone marrow

Upper jaw

BALEEN
About 400 stringy plates of baleen, or "whalebone," hang from the upper jaw like a giant sieve. After every mouthful, the whale licks them on the inside and swallows anything and everything that's been trapped there.

Blubber

TONGUE
Almost bare of taste buds, the whale's four-ton tongue forces water in and out of the mouth and food down the throat.

Krill   *Lower jaw*

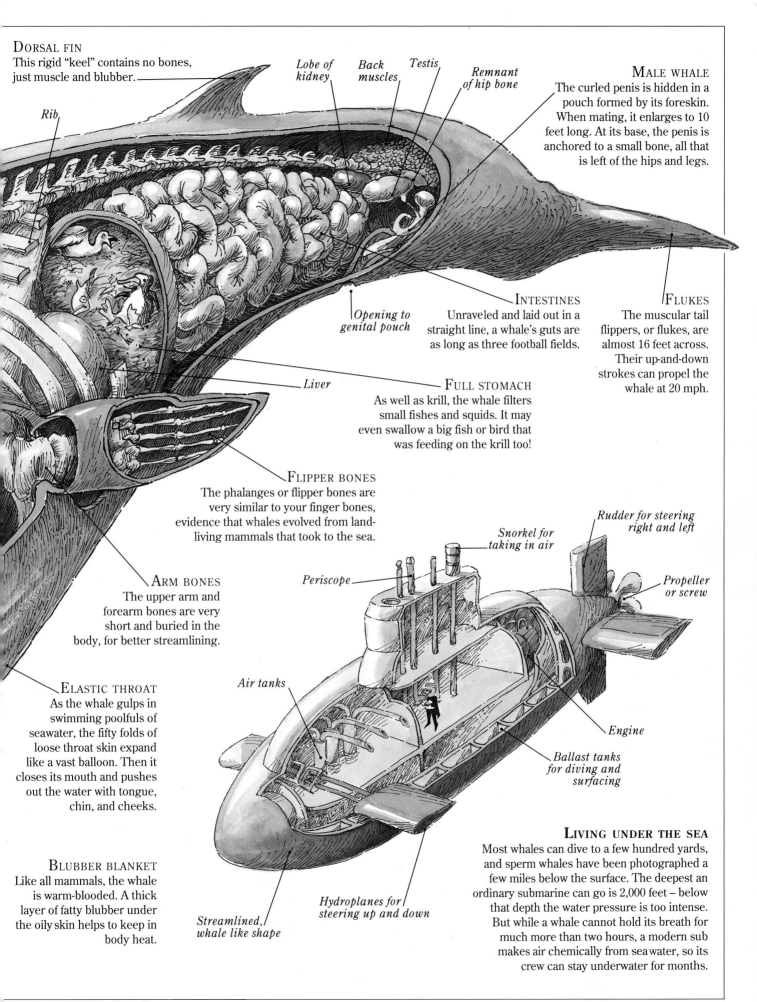

DORSAL FIN
This rigid "keel" contains no bones, just muscle and blubber.

Rib

Lobe of kidney

Back muscles

Testis

Remnant of hip bone

MALE WHALE
The curled penis is hidden in a pouch formed by its foreskin. When mating, it enlarges to 10 feet long. At its base, the penis is anchored to a small bone, all that is left of the hips and legs.

Opening to genital pouch

INTESTINES
Unraveled and laid out in a straight line, a whale's guts are as long as three football fields.

FLUKES
The muscular tail flippers, or flukes, are almost 16 feet across. Their up-and-down strokes can propel the whale at 20 mph.

Liver

FULL STOMACH
As well as krill, the whale filters small fishes and squids. It may even swallow a big fish or bird that was feeding on the krill too!

FLIPPER BONES
The phalanges or flipper bones are very similar to your finger bones, evidence that whales evolved from land-living mammals that took to the sea.

Rudder for steering right and left

Snorkel for taking in air

Periscope

Propeller or screw

ARM BONES
The upper arm and forearm bones are very short and buried in the body, for better streamlining.

Air tanks

ELASTIC THROAT
As the whale gulps in swimming poolfuls of seawater, the fifty folds of loose throat skin expand like a vast balloon. Then it closes its mouth and pushes out the water with tongue, chin, and cheeks.

Engine

Ballast tanks for diving and surfacing

LIVING UNDER THE SEA
Most whales can dive to a few hundred yards, and sperm whales have been photographed a few miles below the surface. The deepest an ordinary submarine can go is 2,000 feet – below that depth the water pressure is too intense. But while a whale cannot hold its breath for much more than two hours, a modern sub makes air chemically from seawater, so its crew can stay underwater for months.

BLUBBER BLANKET
Like all mammals, the whale is warm-blooded. A thick layer of fatty blubber under the oily skin helps to keep in body heat.

Streamlined, whale like shape

Hydroplanes for steering up and down

Mountain Gorilla

Sadly, the massive, muscular mountain gorilla is one of the world's rarest mammals. Only a few hundred survive in the high tropical forests of Central Africa, where they try to munch juicy leaves and stems in peace. The giant vegetarians' only predators are their closest relatives, humans, who shoot them and turn their huge body parts into illegal trophies. The insides of the gorilla are very similar to ours. The main differences are in the skull, which holds a brain only a quarter the volume of our own, and the hips, which are built for moving about on all fours rather than walking upright.

Bowlegs
The curved femur (thighbone) means the gorilla has a more bowlegged stance than a human.

Bent hips
Seen from the side, the long hipbone almost forms a right angle with the vertical thigh and the horizontal backbone.

Barrel chest
The gorilla's ribs curve farther forward than our own, giving it a deeper, barrel-shaped chest.

Spines on vertebrae

Left femur

Ovaries

Growing gorilla
This pregnant gorilla has a 5-month-old fetus in her uterus (womb). In 4 months time, she will give birth to a 4½ lb. baby. The newborn gorilla will be helpless, but will begin to crawl after 10 weeks and walk after 8 months.

Thigh muscles
Like a human, almost half of a gorilla's body weight is muscle. This means a large female carries 90 lbs. of muscle, a large male almost twice as much.

Hairy fact
Although gorillas look much furrier than humans, they have around the same number of hairs as we do. Theirs are just much longer, all over the body.

Uterus

Umbilical cord

Oviduct

Intercostal (inter-rib) muscles

Stomach

Base of tibia (main shinbone)

Base of fibula

Toenails

Metatarsals (sole bones)

Phalanges (toe bones)

Grasping feet
The gorilla has four thumbs, two on its hands and two on its feet, too. It can grip branches between its big toe and other toes. This ability is even greater in its close cousin, the chimp.

8

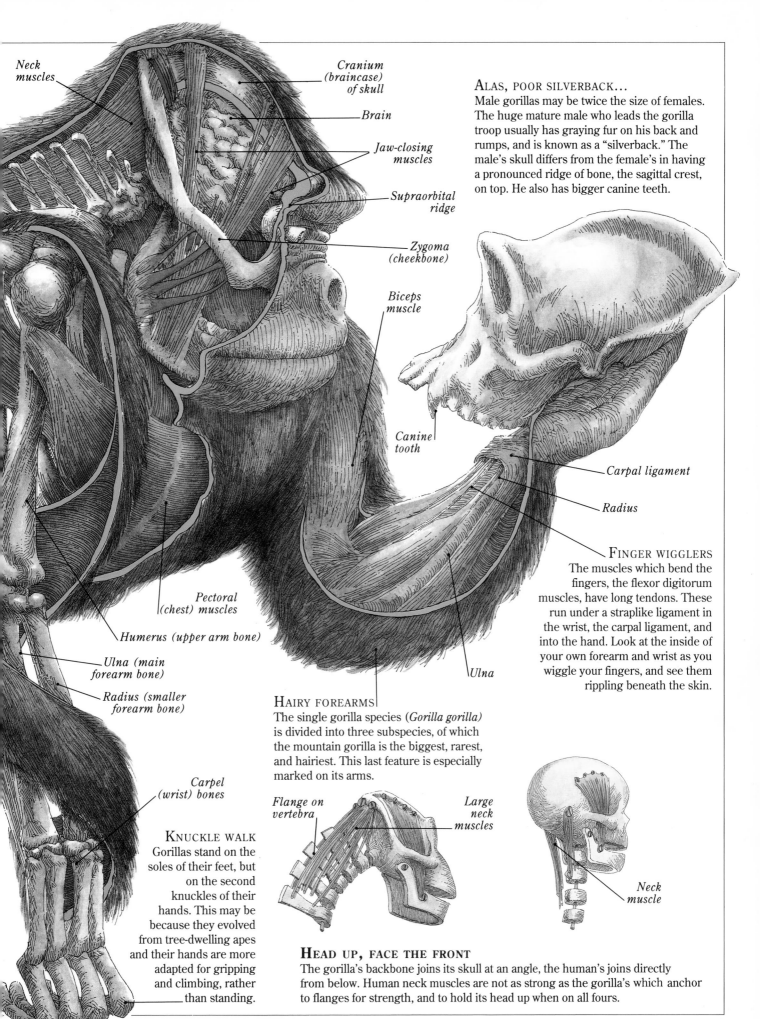

Neck muscles

Cranium (braincase) of skull

Brain

Jaw-closing muscles

Supraorbital ridge

Zygoma (cheekbone)

Biceps muscle

Canine tooth

Pectoral (chest) muscles

Humerus (upper arm bone)

Ulna (main forearm bone)

Radius (smaller forearm bone)

Carpel (wrist) bones

Carpal ligament

Radius

Ulna

ALAS, POOR SILVERBACK...

Male gorillas may be twice the size of females. The huge mature male who leads the gorilla troop usually has graying fur on his back and rumps, and is known as a "silverback." The male's skull differs from the female's in having a pronounced ridge of bone, the sagittal crest, on top. He also has bigger canine teeth.

FINGER WIGGLERS

The muscles which bend the fingers, the flexor digitorum muscles, have long tendons. These run under a straplike ligament in the wrist, the carpal ligament, and into the hand. Look at the inside of your own forearm and wrist as you wiggle your fingers, and see them rippling beneath the skin.

HAIRY FOREARMS

The single gorilla species (*Gorilla gorilla*) is divided into three subspecies, of which the mountain gorilla is the biggest, rarest, and hairiest. This last feature is especially marked on its arms.

Flange on vertebra

Large neck muscles

Neck muscle

KNUCKLE WALK

Gorillas stand on the soles of their feet, but on the second knuckles of their hands. This may be because they evolved from tree-dwelling apes and their hands are more adapted for gripping and climbing, rather than standing.

HEAD UP, FACE THE FRONT

The gorilla's backbone joins its skull at an angle, the human's joins directly from below. Human neck muscles are not as strong as the gorilla's which anchor to flanges for strength, and to hold its head up when on all fours.

DROMEDARY CAMEL

ORIGINALLY DOMESTICATED FOR ITS MEAT, milk, and hair, the camel soon became a beast of burden, too. It has served people for around 5,000 years. Apart from the famous hump, the camel's insides are like other mammals. It is the camel's overall shape and strange body chemistry that make it such a good traveler and desert survivor.

NECK VERTEBRAE
Like its close relatives, the llamas and alpacas, the camel has a long and very bendy neck, ideal for craning into trees and shrubs for food. It contains the standard seven cervical (neck) vertebrae found in all mammals, from mice to giraffes.

Sinus (air space) in skull

Long eyelashes

Parotid (near-the-ear) salivary gland

Sublingual (under-the-tongue) salivary gland

Esophagus (gullet)

CAMEL SPIT
Like most mammals, the camel has three pairs of salivary glands. If threatened, it may spit its saliva with great force.

Mandible (lower jaw)

Palate (roof of mouth)

Submandibular (under-the-jaw) salivary gland

BLOWING BUBBLE
At the rear of the palate is a curious flap of skin known as the dulaa. In the mating season, the male spends a lot of time inflating his and blowing it out of his mouth, like a piece of bubble gum.

Throat

Trachea (windpipe)

FURRY INSULATION
Long, shaggy fur protects the camel from the scorching heat of the noonday sun and the often intense cold of the desert night. On hot days, the camel's body temperature can rise from 93 to 104° F before it starts to sweat. This saves precious water.

Woolly mat shades from sun

Extra fuel

Air filter

High clearance

WATER SUPPLY
The camel does not store water in its stomach. It survives droughts by producing very dry droppings and a small amount of urine, and can withstand losing up to a quarter of its weight in water. When thirsty, it can drink up to 26 gallons of water in a few minutes.

Wide wheels

DESERT DESIGN
The "dune buggy", like the camel, is designed for travel in sandy, inhospitable areas. Wide tires spread its weight to stop the vehicle from sinking, while a high clearance keeps the body up even when the going gets soft. Like the camel's hairy nostrils and long eyelashes, the air filter keeps windblown sand out of the engine. The extra fuel store allows long journeys.

Wide-splayed foot

Vertebrae of spine

Lung

Scapula (shoulder blade)

Heart

THE MYSTERY OF THE HUMP
The legend that the camel stores water in its hump is untrue. Most of the hump is adipose tissue – better known as fat. A camel with a small hump has not eaten for some time and has been living off this fatty food supply.

Rear stomach chamber

Pelvis (hipbone)

Hip joint

Intestine

Stomach

Esophagus

Femur

Thigh muscles

Fused tibia and fibula

Humerus (upper foreleg bone)

LONG LEGS
The lack of "tensor skin" where the legs join the body, at the shoulders and hips, make the beast look even more long legged than it is. An average dromedary is slightly over 6 ½ feet high at the hump.

MILK GLANDS
A well-fed female camel produces 6 quarts of nourishing milk from her mammary glands each day.

Metatarsal (sole) bones

FUSED BONES
The foreleg bones, the radius and ulna, are fused (joined together).

Nerve

NOT AN ELBOW
What looks like the camel's elbow is really its wrist.

Metacarpal bones inside long "palm"

SOFT-SHOE SHUFFLE
The camel's weight is spread farther by a soft, fatty pad under the hoof. Camels are the only hoofed mammals that have these pads.

Tendons

Toe muscle

SWAYING GAIT
A working camel can stride 19 miles a day with a load of 220 lbs. It has a peculiar gait, lifting both legs on one side at the same time, swaying to and fro as it trots.

Twin hooves

Fat pad

AFRICAN ELEPHANT

THE LARGEST LIVING LAND ANIMAL, the enormous elephant may weigh over five and a half tons – the same as 150 ten-year-old children. This great bulk is held up by massive bones that are almost too heavy to be moved by the muscles attached to them. Before and during the Ice Ages, dozens of species of elephant lumbered across the earth. Some of them were even bigger than the two species, the Asian and African, that survive today.

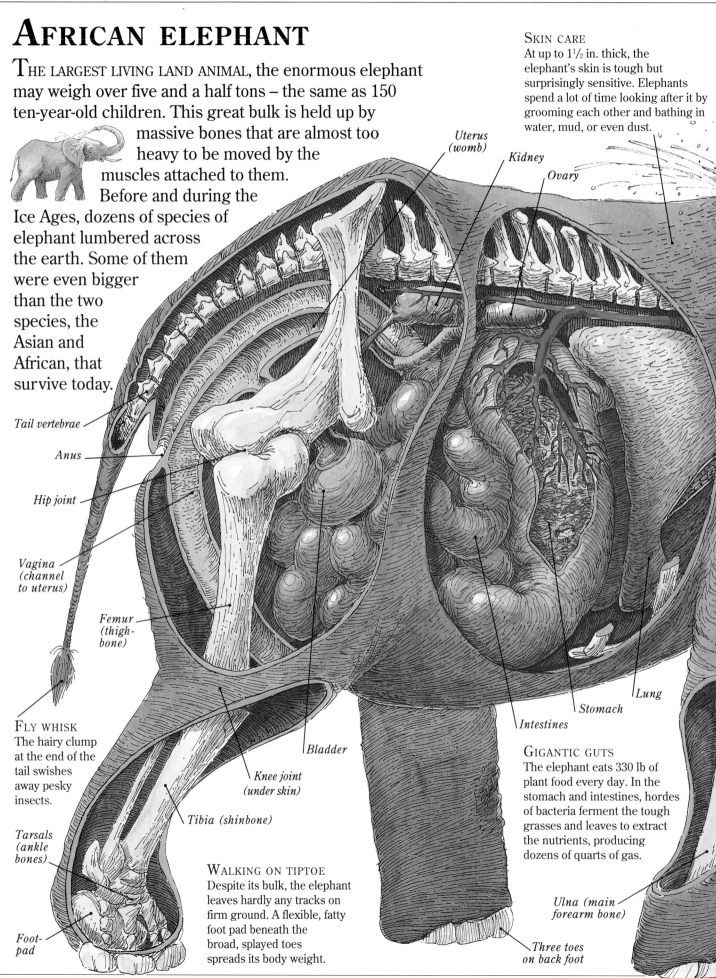

SKIN CARE
At up to 1½ in. thick, the elephant's skin is tough but surprisingly sensitive. Elephants spend a lot of time looking after it by grooming each other and bathing in water, mud, or even dust.

Uterus (womb)

Kidney

Ovary

Tail vertebrae

Anus

Hip joint

Vagina (channel to uterus)

Femur (thigh-bone)

FLY WHISK
The hairy clump at the end of the tail swishes away pesky insects.

Tarsals (ankle bones)

Foot-pad

Knee joint (under skin)

Tibia (shinbone)

Bladder

WALKING ON TIPTOE
Despite its bulk, the elephant leaves hardly any tracks on firm ground. A flexible, fatty foot pad beneath the broad, splayed toes spreads its body weight.

Lung

Stomach

Intestines

GIGANTIC GUTS
The elephant eats 330 lb of plant food every day. In the stomach and intestines, hordes of bacteria ferment the tough grasses and leaves to extract the nutrients, producing dozens of quarts of gas.

Ulna (main forearm bone)

Three toes on back foot

12

SHOWER TIME
The elephant cannot drink through its trunk. It sucks up water, then squirts it into its mouth – or over its back, for a cooling shower.

Sensitive skin and hairs

Blood vessels in ear

Air holes lighten skull bone

FIFTH LIMB
Six and a half feet long, the trunk is a fusion of the elephant's upper lip and nose. It can reach to the ground or high into branches, pick up a tree or an egg, smell and caress friends and pulverize enemies.

Windpipe

Nasal tubes

100,000 muscle fibers in trunk

TEETH . . .
The huge, deep-rooted teeth grind tough plant stems to a pulp. There are three premolars and three molars on either side. As they wear away and fall out, they are replaced from behind.

. . . AND MORE TEETH
Tusks are hugely enlarged incisor (front) teeth. They are made of ivory, a mixture of dentine, cartilage, and calcium minerals. Both sexes use them to dig for food and water, lever bark off trees, and impress rivals and mates.

AFRICAN OR ASIAN?
African elephants have much bigger ears than their Asian cousins.

Rib

Heart

Sternum (breastbone)

WALKING SPEED
Elephants move about as fast as we do. They stroll along at 2-4 mph, and a charging bull (male) has been timed at 25 mph, as fast as the fleetest human sprinter.

Humerus (upper arm bone)

Four toes on front foot

Warmed air out

Flapping motion of ears keeps air moving over them

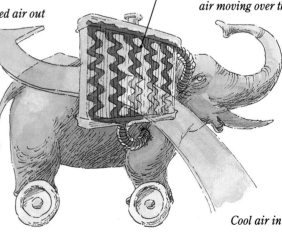

Cool air in

COOLING EARS
The huge ears are richly supplied with blood, bringing warmth from deep in the body. As the ears flap in the breeze, they lose heat, keeping the elephant cool in the same way that a car's radiator keeps its engine cool.

BROWN BAT

ONLY THREE GROUPS OF ANIMALS have
truly conquered the air: insects, birds, and bats.
Bats are amazingly successful, making up a
quarter of the 4,000 species of mammal. Most of
them are insect eaters that fly at dusk or night,
"seeing" in the dark by an astonishingly accurate
system of sound-radar called echolocation.

Though the bat looks superficially like a
bird, closer examination reveals a typical
furry mammal's body. Unlike other
mammals, its arms or
forelimbs have
evolved into
wings of skin
and bone.

FLEXIBLE AIR MOVER
The bat's wing membrane, or
patagium, consists of woven straps
of muscular and elastic fibers
sandwiched between two stretchy
layers of skin. The fibers keep the
wing taut in flight, and fold it up
neatly when the bat roosts.

Third finger

Second or index finger

Hairless wing surface

Radius (forearm bone)

Elbow

Humerus (upper arm bone)

Flight muscles

Carpals (wrist bones)

CLAMBERING CLAW
The bat's thumb has
become a useful claw for
clambering around the
roost, grooming, and in
some cases holding food.

IN-FLIGHT COMPUTER
From the pattern of echoes it
hears, the bat's brain works
out the distance, speed, and
direction of its prey, dozens
of times each second.

Spinal cord

RADAR RECEIVERS
The ears swivel to
pinpoint the direction of
sound waves reflected
from nearby objects. The
system is so sensitive
that a bat can locate a
single hair from more
than three feet away.

Tragus (specialized earlobe)

Skull

Esophagus

Trachea (windpipe)

Clavicle (collarbone)

SOUND SHAPERS
High-pitched cheeps from the larynx
(voice box) are amplified by the sinus
cavities in the skull and then focused
and emitted through the nostrils.

Nostril

SOUNDS OF SILENCE
The bat's larynx makes more
than 200 squeaks and clicks
each second. These are
"ultrasonic," meaning they are
so high in pitch that human
ears cannot detect them.

INSECT IMPALERS
The small, pointed teeth grip and
crunch through the prey's body casing.

Mandible (lower jaw)

14

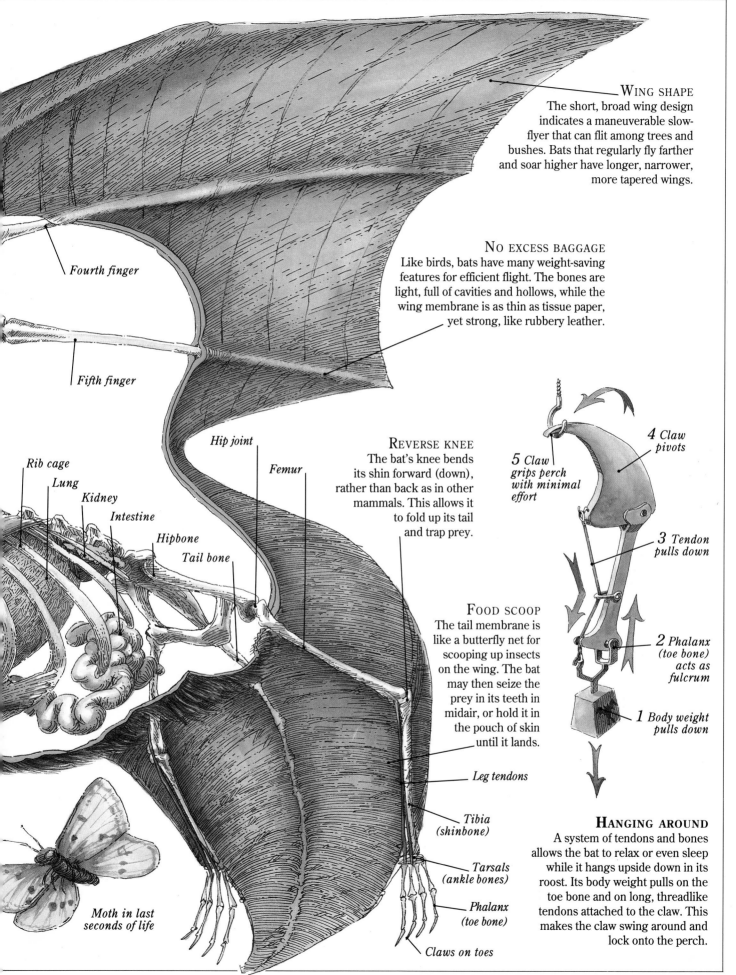

WING SHAPE
The short, broad wing design indicates a maneuverable slow-flyer that can flit among trees and bushes. Bats that regularly fly farther and soar higher have longer, narrower, more tapered wings.

Fourth finger

Fifth finger

NO EXCESS BAGGAGE
Like birds, bats have many weight-saving features for efficient flight. The bones are light, full of cavities and hollows, while the wing membrane is as thin as tissue paper, yet strong, like rubbery leather.

Hip joint

Femur

REVERSE KNEE
The bat's knee bends its shin forward (down), rather than back as in other mammals. This allows it to fold up its tail and trap prey.

5 Claw grips perch with minimal effort

4 Claw pivots

3 Tendon pulls down

Rib cage

Lung

Kidney

Intestine

Hipbone

Tail bone

FOOD SCOOP
The tail membrane is like a butterfly net for scooping up insects on the wing. The bat may then seize the prey in its teeth in midair, or hold it in the pouch of skin until it lands.

2 Phalanx (toe bone) acts as fulcrum

1 Body weight pulls down

Leg tendons

Tibia (shinbone)

HANGING AROUND
A system of tendons and bones allows the bat to relax or even sleep while it hangs upside down in its roost. Its body weight pulls on the toe bone and on long, threadlike tendons attached to the claw. This makes the claw swing around and lock onto the perch.

Tarsals (ankle bones)

Moth in last seconds of life

Phalanx (toe bone)

Claws on toes

15

GRAY KANGAROO

A COAT OF SOFT GRAY FUR and mammary glands that produce milk to feed the young make the kangaroo a mammal.
But the structure of the reproductive system marks out the kangaroo as a particular kind of mammal – a marsupial. One main difference is in the womb. A female marsupial does not have a placenta – the special organ that nourishes the developing young in the womb, and which is found in bats, whales, dogs, cats, monkeys, humans, and other placental mammals. But she does have a marsupium – a pocket or pouch. The newborn youngster creeps into this and stays there, suckling milk and growing in safety.

LEAPING MUSCLES
The huge muscles of the hip, calf, and shin propel the 'roo forward in great bounds. Kangaroos can jump as high as 4½ feet, but a big male or "boomer" can clear fences almost 10 feet high.

GUTS
All kangaroos, and their close relatives the wallabies, are herbivores. The large sacculated (multi-chambered) stomach digests coarse grass, leaves, and other vegetable matter.

Ribs

Vertebrae (backbones)

Top of pelvis

KNEES STRAIGHT
The powerful knee-straightening muscle is securely anchored to the upper part of the pelvis, or hipbone.

THE BOUNCY U
The kangaroo's body, legs, and huge feet form a sideways U shape, which closes and opens as the animal bounds. Its muscles, tendons, and joints are also very springy and store energy, like stretched elastic. So the 'roo can "bounce" along with the minimum of effort.

Femur (thigh-bone)

SEATING, BALANCING, AND STEERING
The muscular tail is more than 3 feet in length. It works as a prop to lean back on when resting, a balancer when bounding, and a counterweight-rudder when changing direction.

Caudal (tail) vertebrae

BABY-IN-WAITING
About five weeks ago, this female kangaroo mated. Now a tiny wormlike baby, about 0.04 ounces in weight, is at the upper part of the uterus, almost ready to be born.

A CUTE PAIR OF EARS
Kangaroos feed mainly at night, using their large ears, and acute sense of hearing, to detect possible danger. They can swivel their ear flaps to pinpoint the direction of sounds. During the day they rest and doze in whatever shade they can find.

GRAY COAT
There are five species of "great kangaroos": the red or marloo, the eastern gray or forester, the western gray or mallee, the wallaroo, and the antelope kangaroo. The gray and red species are the largest. Big males grow 6½ feet high and weigh 150 pounds. The grays differ from the reds in coat color (which is not always clear-cut) and also . . .

FURRY NOSE
. . . by their furry noses. The red kangaroo lacks the fine, downy fur between its nostrils.

Skull

Mandible (lower jaw-bone)

Esophagus (gullet)

Trachea (windpipe)

Scapula (shoulder blade)

TWO FOREPAWS
The five-clawed front feet are used when the kangaroo moves slowly. It places them down and then brings the back legs forward on either side, just like its great competitor in the Australian outback, the rabbit.

JOEY AT HOME
The young kangaroo is called a joey. It is now nine months old and ready to leave the safety of the mother's pouch. Within days the new baby in the uterus will be born and undertake an incredible journey, crawling to its mother's pouch and attaching itself to one of the four nipples there.

BIG-FOOT
The great gray kangaroo's scientific name, *Macropus,* means "big foot." Instead of having five toes on each foot, as we do, kangaroos have four – the first is missing, the next two are small, and the last two very large.

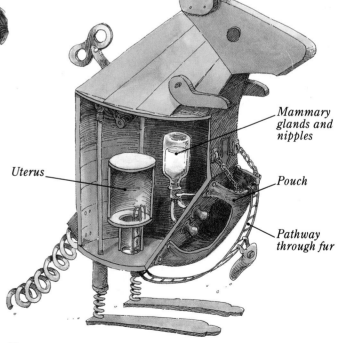

Mammary glands and nipples

Uterus

Pouch

Pathway through fur

THE INCREDIBLE JOURNEY
At birth the joey is barely ¾ inch long. It has two oarlike front limbs, but little else. It cannot see or hear. Yet it manages to "row" from the birth opening, through the maternal fur, around its mother's belly, and into the pouch – an amazing five-minute obstacle course. In the pouch, the nourishing milk is waiting.

EAGLE OWL

A YOUNG TAWNY OWL leaves its perch and swoops silently through the dusk, across the field toward a rustle in the bushes. Without warning a bigger shadow envelops it; great talons pierce its body, and huge wings haul it, dying, skyward. The tawny owl, itself a formidable predator, has fallen victim to the speed and power of an eagle owl. Owls have features typical of a bird, such as hollow bones and an extensive system of air spaces among the body organs. The air spaces are weight-saving, and also help the bird to breathe efficiently by creating a one-way flow of air through their lungs.

NIGHT-SIGHTS
Most owls are nocturnal and have huge eyes to gather as much light as possible. The fields of vision of the two eyes overlap considerably, giving binocular or 3-D sight (as in ourselves). This enables the owl to see depth and judge distance more accurately.

Iris

Retina

Lens

Maxilla (upper jaw)

Mandible (lower jaw)

OFFSET EARS
The ear opening in one side of the owl's skull is slightly lower than the opening on the other side. This may help the owl to pinpoint the direction of sounds. The facial disks of feathers also channel sounds toward the ear openings.

FOUND BY SOUND, STRIKE BY SIGHT
A hungry owl listens intently for possible victims, and turns its head to equalize the sounds coming into each ear. It then looks straight at the prey, which it can eventually make out in the gloom with its light sensitive eyes. Sight takes over as the owl dives and grabs its meal.

WHAT'S THIS EAR?
The "ears" are simply tufts of extralong feathers. The real ears are on the sides of the head.

WING BONES
Each forelimb bone has its equivalent in a mammal or reptile. Evolution has reshaped them for flapping flight, not walking.

Thumb

Carpals (wrist)

Radius and ulna (forearm bones)

Elbow

Humerus (upper arm bone)

Trachea (windpipe)

Esophagus (gullet)

Pectoral (flight) muscles

Offset ears

Both eyes face forward

TOO BIG TO TURN
Owl eyes are such a tight fit in their sockets that they cannot swivel. So the owl must twist or nod its whole head to look around. Its cervical (neck) vertebrae are very flexible – the bird can rotate its head 180º to look directly behind itself!

Feather root

FLIGHT
FLIGHT
The soft-edged feathers make hardly any noise as the owl flies. The large strong feathers near the wingtip are the primaries, giving most of the lift in flight. The eagle owl has a wingspan of more than three feet.

Pygostyle (tail vertebrae)

Intestines

PACKED INTO A PELLET
Unlike many eagles and hawks, which tear their food to bits with beak and claws, owls usually swallow theirs whole, head-first. The hard, indigestible parts like bones, skin, birds' beaks, claws, and fish scales are compressed into a neat pellet by part of the stomach. Some 10-15 hours after swallowing, the owl regurgitates (coughs up) the pelleted leftovers.

Femur (thigh-bone)

Knee

ONE-WAY FLOW
Unlike the tidal "ebb-and-flow" system of mammals, air flows mainly in one direction through birds' lungs, from one set of air sacs to another. This means less dead space and more efficient oxygen absorption.

Tibia (shin-bone)

False knee

FEATHERED LEGS
Soft, flexible feathers cover most of the owl's lower limbs, making it seem shorter-legged than it really is. The same smooth "feathering" obscures the owl's long, bendy neck and gives it a neckless appearance.

Tarsometatarsus

Digits

DEADLY TALONS
As the owl contacts its victim, it throws back its head and strikes with its talons. The long, curved claws spear and squeeze the prey, killing small animals outright.

19

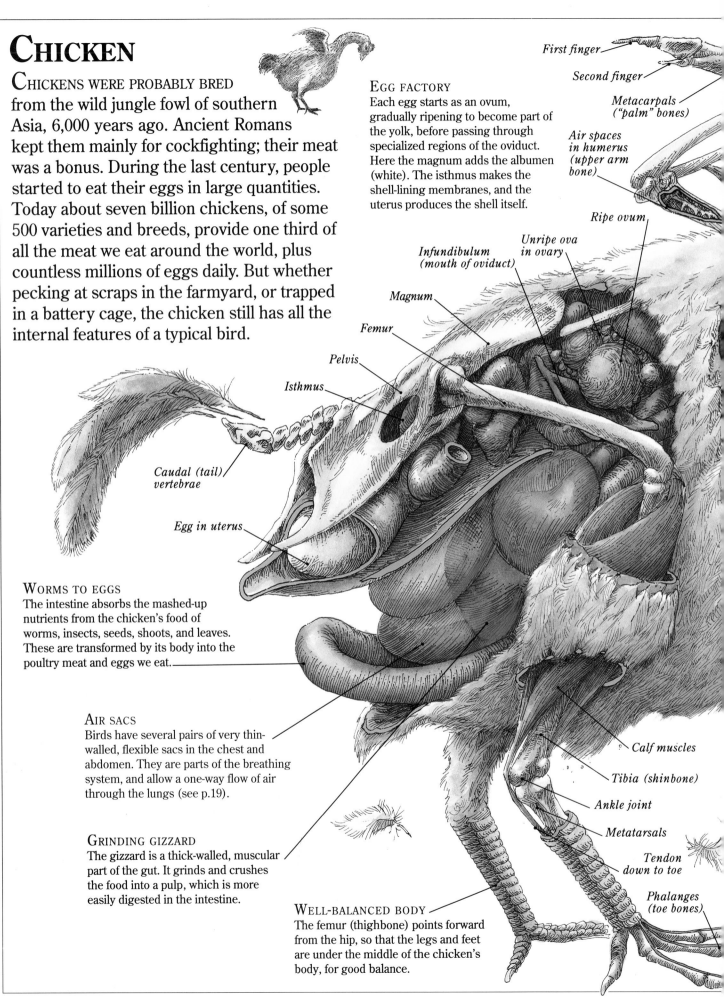

CHICKEN

CHICKENS WERE PROBABLY BRED from the wild jungle fowl of southern Asia, 6,000 years ago. Ancient Romans kept them mainly for cockfighting; their meat was a bonus. During the last century, people started to eat their eggs in large quantities. Today about seven billion chickens, of some 500 varieties and breeds, provide one third of all the meat we eat around the world, plus countless millions of eggs daily. But whether pecking at scraps in the farmyard, or trapped in a battery cage, the chicken still has all the internal features of a typical bird.

EGG FACTORY
Each egg starts as an ovum, gradually ripening to become part of the yolk, before passing through specialized regions of the oviduct. Here the magnum adds the albumen (white). The isthmus makes the shell-lining membranes, and the uterus produces the shell itself.

First finger

Second finger

Metacarpals ("palm" bones)

Air spaces in humerus (upper arm bone)

Ripe ovum

Unripe ova in ovary

Infundibulum (mouth of oviduct)

Magnum

Femur

Pelvis

Isthmus

Caudal (tail) vertebrae

Egg in uterus

WORMS TO EGGS
The intestine absorbs the mashed-up nutrients from the chicken's food of worms, insects, seeds, shoots, and leaves. These are transformed by its body into the poultry meat and eggs we eat.

AIR SACS
Birds have several pairs of very thin-walled, flexible sacs in the chest and abdomen. They are parts of the breathing system, and allow a one-way flow of air through the lungs (see p.19).

GRINDING GIZZARD
The gizzard is a thick-walled, muscular part of the gut. It grinds and crushes the food into a pulp, which is more easily digested in the intestine.

WELL-BALANCED BODY
The femur (thighbone) points forward from the hip, so that the legs and feet are under the middle of the chicken's body, for good balance.

Calf muscles

Tibia (shinbone)

Ankle joint

Metatarsals

Tendon down to toe

Phalanges (toe bones)

Thumb

Carpals
(wrist)

Ulna

Radius

Lung

Neck muscles
and tendons

Neck muscles
and tendons

Back of skull

Cervical (neck)
vertebrae

Trachea
(windpipe)

NO CROPS IN THIS CROP
The lower part of the esophagus (gullet) forms the crop. Its elastic walls expand to hold seeds and other foods the chicken happens to come upon.

COMB
The hen's comb is not as flamboyant as the roosters. He uses it to impress her when courting.

LIGHTWEIGHT BEAK
The lightweight, horn-covered beak has replaced heavy teeth and jawbones, making it easier for the bird to fly. The beak pecks and tears, but cannot chew food. The gizzard (opposite) does this.

NOSTRILS
The chicken finds food partly by sight, and by using its sense of smell, as it pecks away at likely looking items on the ground.

Clavicle
(collarbone)

Coracoid

Rib

Sternum
(breastbone)

Keel of sternum

KEEL
The large sternum has a flange called the keel or carina, which anchors the powerful flight muscles we know as "chicken breast." The clavicles form a V shape known wistfully as the "wishbone."

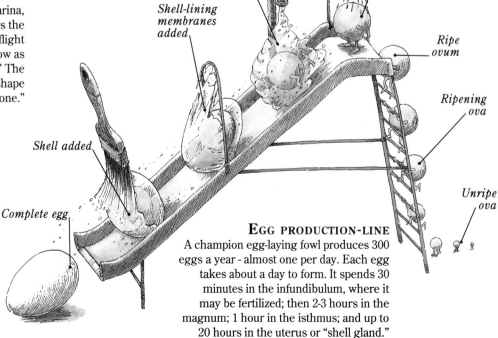

Fertilization by
rooster's sperm

Albumen
added

Shell-lining
membranes
added

Ripe
ovum

Ripening
ova

Shell added

Complete egg

Unripe
ova

CLAWS
Each bird toe is tipped with a claw. Chickens use them mainly for scratching for food and perching. Hunting birds have large hooked talons.

EGG PRODUCTION-LINE
A champion egg-laying fowl produces 300 eggs a year - almost one per day. Each egg takes about a day to form. It spends 30 minutes in the infundibulum, where it may be fertilized; then 2-3 hours in the magnum; 1 hour in the isthmus; and up to 20 hours in the uterus or "shell gland."

RATTLESNAKE

In the dry brush country of North America, few sounds are more hair-raising than the harsh buzz of the diamondback rattlesnake. Under its scaly exterior this deadly snake has all the usual body parts of a land vertebrate – skeleton, heart, intestines, liver – with a few additions, such as poison glands and nearly two hundred extra vertebrae. But to fit into the tubular body, some pairs of organs (such as the kidneys) are offset one behind the other, rather than being side by side. In other cases, one member of the organ pair (like the lungs) has shrunk, or even disappeared.

LAST WEEK'S MEAL
A fairly large snake like the rattler only needs to feed once every week or two. Even then the stomach is still digesting the bones of the last victim.

SHEDDING SKIN
A rattlesnake sheds its skin about three times a year, replacing it with a new, larger skin beneath. This is the only way the snake can grow, as its scales cannot enlarge or multiply once they harden.

A REAL MOUTHFUL
The snake has no molar teeth and cannot chew its food. Instead, it swallows its prey whole, working its jaws around the head and down the body with successive swallows.

SNAKE STARE
Snakes never blink, because their transparent eyelids are always closed.

Fang-erecting muscle

Poison duct

Eye orbit

Maxillary bone

Fang

Jaw-raising muscles

Spinal cord   *Esophagus*

Right lung

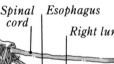

Liver

Heart

BLOOD BREAKDOWN
The venom in the rattler's large poison glands is hemotoxic. It attacks the victim's blood cells, causing massive internal bleeding and bruising.

Skeleton of prey

Ligament connecting lower jaw halves

Dentary bone

Extra jaw hinge

Main part of maxilla (lower jaw)

LONG LUNG
The right lung extends forward and wraps around the windpipe, where it is called the tracheal lung.

Start of esophagus

Sperm duct from testis

STAGGERED KIDNEYS
Like the testes, the kidneys are one in front of the other, the right being farthest forward. They make urine crystals, which are expelled with the feces.

TESTES
This male's testes are much enlarged, showing he is ready to mate.

Intestine

A ROW OF OLD TAILS
Each time the rattler sheds its skin, the cone-shaped tip of the tail is left behind. A groove around its upper part hooks loosely into the base of the last tail end. This is how the rattle forms.

Rear end of left kidney

Inturned base

Groove

LEFT LUNG
The left lung, much smaller than the right, is linked to the windpipe by a tube, the bronchus.

Bronchus

SLITHERY SCALES
The snake's belly scales slide forward and backward in waves, their edges gripping tiny bumps and pits in the surface to pull the snake along.

THIN FAT
Reptiles do not store excess food as layers of fat around the body, like mammals, but as two long threadlike organs called fat bodies.

Fangs swing forward

PLENTY OF BACKBONE
The average snake has more than 200 vertebrae, compared to 26 in an adult human and only 8 or 9 in a frog.

Connecting ligaments stretch

Jaw joints stretch

Extra jaw joint flexes

Fangs fold upward

WINDPIPE
During the swallowing process, which may take more than an hour, the muscular windpipe pushes forward along the bottom of the mouth so the reptile can still breathe.

OPEN WIDE
A snake's lower jaws contain hinges and are connected to the skull by extremely elastic ligaments. These unique structures allow it to open wide and swallow prey bigger than its own head.

AT REST
Normally the fangs, which pivot forward when the snake strikes, are folded flat against the roof of the mouth. The ligaments between the various jaw and facial bones keep the head slim and flat.

GIANT TORTOISE

MORE THAN 200 MILLION YEARS AGO, as the first dinosaurs stalked the earth, chelonians (tortoises and turtles) lumbered onto the land. These remarkably ancient animals  have forsaken speed and agility for three layers of heavy wraparound armor. Hungry predators need strong jaws indeed to crack through the outer scutes, the bones of the carapace in the middle, and the usual ribs and other skeletal bones on the inside.

Neck muscles

SCALY SKIN
Like all reptiles, the tortoise has a strong, scaly covering of skin. This sheds in patches as the creature grows, scraping away old skin and scales with its clawed legs.

Five-clawed front foot

SCUTES
There are about 54 of these thin outer plates (16 on the underside), fixed to each other at their edges and to the bony plates below. They are made of tough, but light, horn.

Vertebra (backbone)

Aorta (main blood vessel)

Right lung

Spinal cord

Esophagus

Trachea

Ear chamber

Scapula

Humerus

Radius

Ulna

Wrist bones

SENSING SCENTS
Food is found mainly by smell. Sniffing with its nostrils in the usual way, the tortoise picks up airborne scents with a special detector in the roof of its mouth, called Jacobson's organ.

Stiff tongue

EAR-BENDING
The jaw-closing muscle runs in a pulleylike groove, to get around the large ear chamber.

TOOTHLESS JAWS
The jaws are covered by a sharp ridge of horny substance. Unable to chew, the tortoise pins its meal down with its front feet, and snips off and swallows a little at a time.

LIFE IN THE SLOW LANE
Built for sturdy lifting power, the legs raise the heavy shell off the ground when walking. A 500 yard dash takes the tortoise about an hour.

Left lung *Rib*

CARAPACE
Under the scutes are a thick set of about 60 plates, made of bone. They form the carapace over the back, and the plastron underneath. The joints in the scutes and carapace do not line up, making the whole casing less likely to crack.

Pelvic (hip) bones

WRAPAROUND RIBS
The backbone and ribs are fastened to the underside of the carapace, helping to reinforce the whole shell. The 10 pairs of ribs wrap around the shoulders and hips for even greater rigidity.

TUCK-AWAY TAIL
The small tail is very flexible, like the neck, and can be tucked under the back of the shell, out of harm's way.

Knee joint

Femur

Walking muscles

Bladder

Calf and shin muscles

IN THE INTESTINE
Like most of its hard-shelled cousins, the tortoise is an omnivore that can eat almost anything. Foods may range from leaves and fruits, to insects, fish, or small animals. Those that are chiefly vegetarian have intestines seven times as long as their shell; in meat-eaters they are half this length.

Stomach

Plastron

Coracoid

Clavicle (collarbone)

STRANGE SHOULDERS
The scapula is fixed to the carapace above, and the clavicle to the plastron below. This makes a stiff shoulder that can only swing forward and backward.

KERATIN CLAWS
The claws, like the scutes, are made of a horny substance keratin (see p.27).

BREATHING IN . . .
The rigid shell means a tortoise cannot expand its rib cage to breathe in. It uses muscles that push aside its intestines and other abdominal organs. These expand into the loose pockets of skin around the bases of the legs.

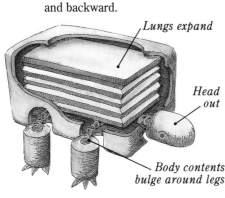

Lungs expand

Head out

Body contents bulge around legs

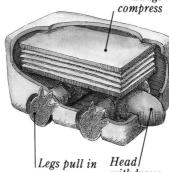

Lungs compress

. . . AND HOLD IT!
When the tortoise pulls into its shell, the legs squash its lungs and other organs — which means it can hardly breathe! Fortunately its body chemistry can cope with a buildup of waste carbon dioxide and lack of oxygen, so hiding doesn't mean suffocating!

Legs pull in *Head withdraws*

NILE CROCODILE

A RELATIVE of those extinct giants, the dinosaurs, this toothy reptile looks like a primeval misfit in the modern world. In fact, the crocodile is one of nature's most successful designs, floating in wait in the river Nile today as it once did in the primordial swamp. Fossils show that its skeleton has barely changed over the past 200 million years, and paleontologists guess the same is true of its flesh and soft parts, which have left no remains. One reason for the croc's survival is the hard scales, which protect and camouflage it. Another is its huge mouth, built to rip chunks out of large prey or swallow smaller victims whole.

SWIM AND STEER
The crocodile swims by lashing its tail from side to side. With its legs bunched up, it is streamlined and goes straight ahead; dropping one leg slightly will make the animal veer to left or right.

ESCAPE TRICK
When threatened, the croc slashes the water with its long, flat tail. This shoots the animal forward, leaving a foaming whirlpool in its wake. It may then dive and turn to lose the molester.

LONG TAIL
The longest reliably recorded croc, an Asian saltwater specimen, measured 28 feet from tail to snout.

Stationary foot

Legs swings

Body arches to right

Body arches to left

Stationary foot

CROC WALK
The crocodile swings its body from side to side as it walks, each stride arching the body into a new S shape.

BRAINY REPTILE
The croc's brain is more advanced than those of most other reptiles. The cortex, the thinking part, is relatively large, and research shows that crocodiles are faster learners than lizards or snakes.

SMELL ORGANS
The olfactory lobes, organs of smell, are outgrowths from the front of the brain.

Neck muscles

Ear opening

Roof of skull

NOSE HOLES
The nostrils, and the eyes and ears are set high on the head. Floating like a harmless old log, the croc can still breathe, smell, look, and listen.

Nasal breathing passage

Olfactory (smell) passage

Hard palate

Skull bone

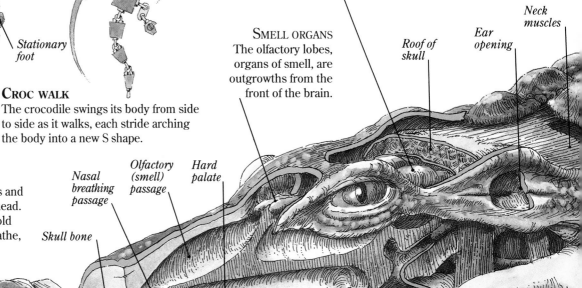

Jaw-closing muscle

THROAT VALVE
These flaps close on diving, so that the croc can eat when submerged without swallowing water.

Replacement tooth

Mature tooth

Maxilla (lower jaw)

Muscle fibers

WELL ARMORED
Like its claws (and your fingernails), the croc's scales are made of a horny protein called keratin, which is formed in the outer layer of the skin, the epidermis. Underneath them are osteoderms, bony plates embedded in the lower layer of skin, the dermis.

TASTY FLESH
Crocs tend to bask in groups of similar-sized individuals. This is because crocodile meat is nourishing, and big crocs have been known to eat smaller crocs.

MUSCLE ANCHORS
The flanges and spines on the vertebrae are anchors for the powerful tail muscles.

LUNGS
Like all reptiles, the crocodile breathes air, and can only hold its breath for a few minutes at a time. Kept underwater, it would drown.

Pelvis (hip bone)

Femur (thigh bone)

Kidney

Front of right lung

Gullet

Main artery

Knee joint

Spinal cord

Intestines

Tibia and fibula (shinbones)

Rib

STOMACH STONES
The pebbles it regularly swallows help grind unchewed food and stabilize the croc when it floats low in the water.

Liver

Humerus

Webbed back toes

DIVIDED HEART
Most reptiles have only one ventricle, the heart's main pumping chamber. But the crocodile's is virtually divided in two, as it is in birds and mammals.

BACK FEET FORWARD
A croc cruising at the surface can escape from danger by spreading its webbed back feet and thrusting them up and forward. This causes it to stop moving forward and sink swiftly from sight.

Aorta (main artery from heart)

Main vein

Scapula (shoulder blade)

Trachea (windpipe)

Unwebbed front toes

27

TRICERATOPS

THIS DINOSAUR DIED 65 MILLION YEARS AGO, so how do we know about its insides? Many well-preserved *Triceratops* bones from North America tell us about its skeleton. Its fossilized teeth and the preserved stomach contents of similar dinosaurs give clues to diet and digestion. Fossilized skin from other dinosaurs, and comparisons with living relatives like crocodiles, help to fill in other parts of the picture. But this reconstruction is still largely informed guesswork.

OL' THREE-HORNED FACE
The name *Triceratops* means "three-horned face," after the two large brow horns, and smaller nose horn. The dinosaur may have used these for defense, charging at molesters like a modern-day rhino. Or it could have locked horns with rivals while competing for the attention of females.

BONY FRILL
The main structure of the frill was formed by backward projections from the parietal and squamosal, two bones of the skull.

WAVY EDGE
Small knobbly lumps of bone, the epoccipitals, gave the frill a wavy edge.

Pectoral girdle (shoulder bones)

Brow horns

NASAL FORAMEN
To save weight, the skull had various holes where firmness was less important.

Nose horn

Nostril

Trachea (windpipe)

Esophagus (gullet)

Elbow joint

Radius

Jaw muscles

Ulna

SNIP-SNIP
An effective snipper for leafy vegetation, the parrotlike "beak" at the tip of the mouth was covered in a hard horny substance.

CUT-CUT
The rows of sharp teeth sliced and cut the vegetable food into smaller pieces.

CHEW-CHEW
A bar of bone at right angles to the main lower jaw, the coronoid process, gave extra anchorage to the strong jaw muscles, used for chewing food.

STUMPY LEGS
Massive legs like columns supported the creature's total weight of over five and a half tons – the same as a large African elephant. Splayed toes spread this weight on the ground.

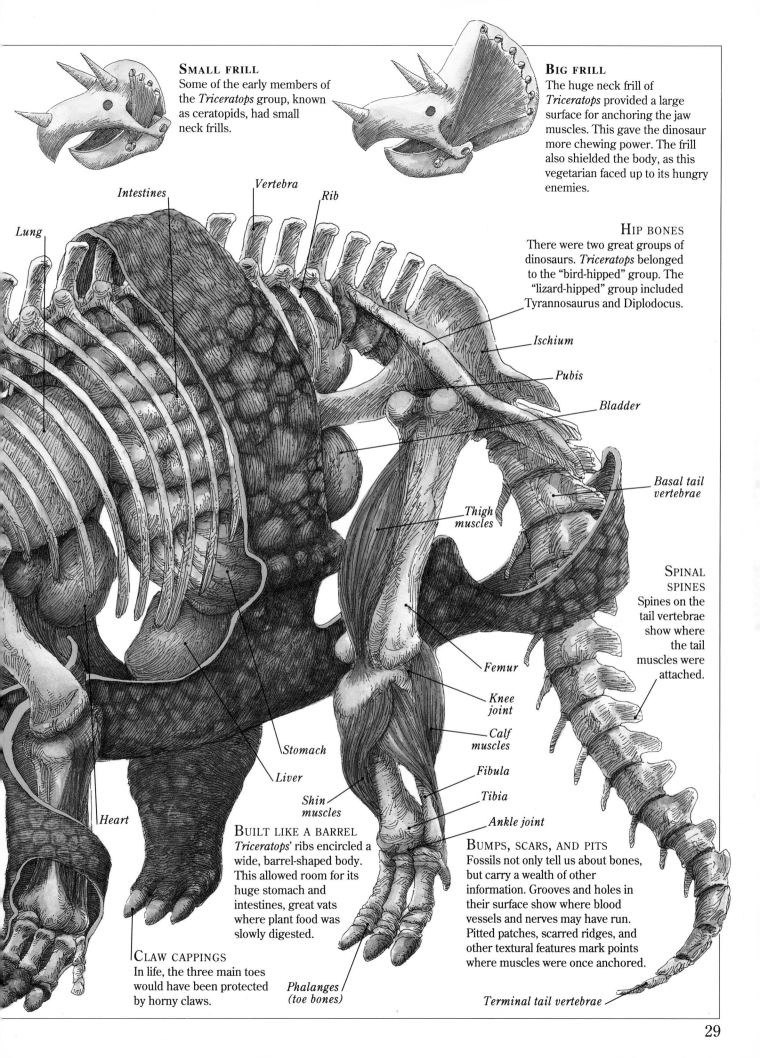

SMALL FRILL
Some of the early members of the *Triceratops* group, known as ceratopids, had small neck frills.

BIG FRILL
The huge neck frill of *Triceratops* provided a large surface for anchoring the jaw muscles. This gave the dinosaur more chewing power. The frill also shielded the body, as this vegetarian faced up to its hungry enemies.

Intestines

Vertebra

Rib

Lung

HIP BONES
There were two great groups of dinosaurs. *Triceratops* belonged to the "bird-hipped" group. The "lizard-hipped" group included Tyrannosaurus and Diplodocus.

Ischium

Pubis

Bladder

Basal tail vertebrae

Thigh muscles

SPINAL SPINES
Spines on the tail vertebrae show where the tail muscles were attached.

Femur

Knee joint

Calf muscles

Stomach

Liver

Fibula

Tibia

Ankle joint

Shin muscles

Heart

BUILT LIKE A BARREL
Triceratops' ribs encircled a wide, barrel-shaped body. This allowed room for its huge stomach and intestines, great vats where plant food was slowly digested.

BUMPS, SCARS, AND PITS
Fossils not only tell us about bones, but carry a wealth of other information. Grooves and holes in their surface show where blood vessels and nerves may have run. Pitted patches, scarred ridges, and other textural features mark points where muscles were once anchored.

CLAW CAPPINGS
In life, the three main toes would have been protected by horny claws.

Phalanges (toe bones)

Terminal tail vertebrae

GREEN FROG

HOME FOR THE TYPICAL FROG is quiet, cool, and damp. The frog is a predator, feeding on worms, beetles, flies, slugs, and similar small creatures. For most of the year, it lurks in the undergrowth, or some other shady place, waiting for food to wander by. But the frog is also an amphibian, and every year it returns to water to breed. Female frogs lay jelly-covered eggs, or spawn, that hatch into tadpoles. The frog has a bony backbone, skeleton, and four limbs. There are only nine or fewer vertebrae in the backbone, and no neck, or tail. The name for the frog group is *Anura*, meaning "tailless."

COMPACT DESIGN
Unlike its enormous legs, the frog's body is short, round, and compact. This reduces the risks of its spine and organs shaking, bending, or twisting too much during a jump, and causing harm.

POISON
A frog's skin contains mucous glands which make its slippery covering, to prevent too much water loss. It also has some poison glands, which ooze a vile-tasting fluid if the frog is attacked.

Lungs

Vertebrae

Pelvis

Kidney

Tailbone

Anus

Ball and socket of hip

Femur

Tibia-fibula

Ankle joint

LIVING ELECTRICITY
In 1780, while working with leg muscles dissected from a dead frog, the Italian scientist, Luigi Galvani, saw that the muscles shortened when touched with certain metals. Later, in about 1800, this led to the invention of the battery by Alessandro Volta.

Webbing between digits

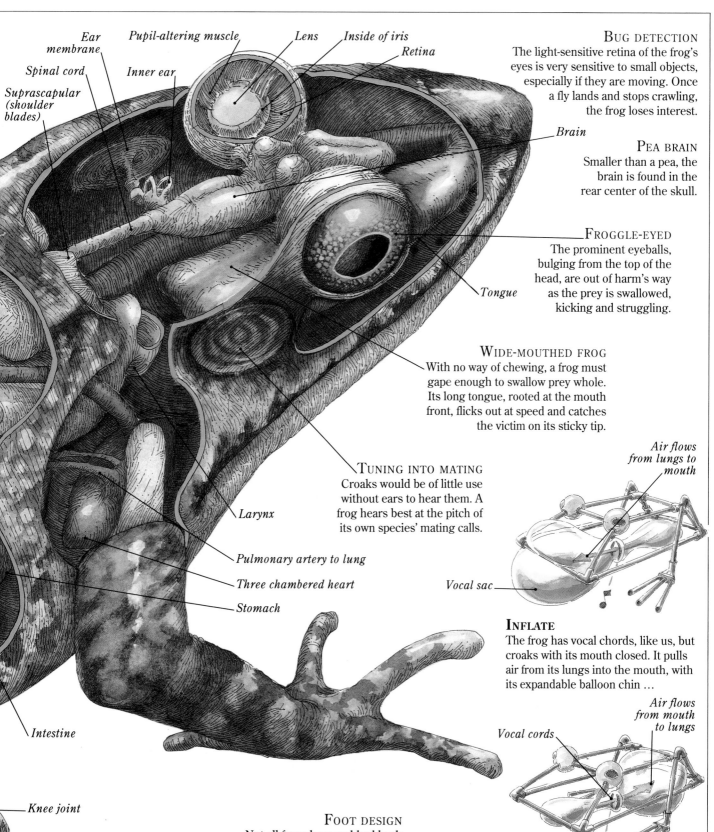

Ear
membrane

Pupil-altering muscle   Lens   Inside of iris

Spinal cord   Inner ear   Retina

Suprascapular
(shoulder
blades)

Brain

BUG DETECTION
The light-sensitive retina of the frog's
eyes is very sensitive to small objects,
especially if they are moving. Once
a fly lands and stops crawling,
the frog loses interest.

PEA BRAIN
Smaller than a pea, the
brain is found in the
rear center of the skull.

FROGGLE-EYED
The prominent eyeballs,
bulging from the top of the
head, are out of harm's way
as the prey is swallowed,
kicking and struggling.

Tongue

WIDE-MOUTHED FROG
With no way of chewing, a frog must
gape enough to swallow prey whole.
Its long tongue, rooted at the mouth
front, flicks out at speed and catches
the victim on its sticky tip.

Air flows
from lungs to
mouth

TUNING INTO MATING
Croaks would be of little use
without ears to hear them. A
frog hears best at the pitch of
its own species' mating calls.

Larynx

Vocal sac

INFLATE
The frog has vocal chords, like us, but
croaks with its mouth closed. It pulls
air from its lungs into the mouth, with
its expandable balloon chin …

Pulmonary artery to lung

Three chambered heart

Stomach

Air flows
from mouth
to lungs

Vocal cords

Intestine

Knee joint

FOOT DESIGN
Not all frogs have webbed back
feet. Some have spade-shaped
lumps for burrowing, others
have splayed suckerlike toes for
gripping leaves. In "flying frogs,"
the webs are so broad that their
owner can glide from tree to
tree, using them as wings.

AND CROAK
… and then forces the air back again,
making the return croak. This is also
how it breathes. Several frogs are
named after what we imagine the
croaks to sound like, such as rifle
frogs, bullfrogs, barking frogs, spring
peepers, and sheep frogs.

GREAT WHITE SHARK

NEVER QUITE AS BIG as it seems in the cinema, the great white is nonetheless a fearsome eating machine. At a mere 20 feet, it is still 32 feet shorter than the largest fish, the whale shark. But while that monster eats nothing but tiny plankton, the great white is a carnivore that occasionally lives up to its reputation as a man-eater.

Sharks and their relatives, skates and rays, are chondrichthyes or "cartilage fishes." They differ from the more numerous osteichthyes, "bony fishes," chiefly in having a skeleton made of cartilage, not bone. Fossils show that the basic shark structure must be successful, as it has remained virtually unchanged for the last 300 million years.

SWIMMING FOR LIFE
Sharks lack the inflatable swim bladder that allows bony fish to control their buoyancy. Most sharks must swim endlessly. If they stop, they sink to the bottom, and may drown from a lack of water flowing over the gills.

Fin rays support fin

First dorsal fin

BACK "BONE"
The vertebrae, shaped like cotton reels and made of cartilage, may be strengthened with calcium minerals, as bone is. Inside are two tunnels down which run the spinal cord and the notocord, a primitive spinal column.

Main swimming muscles

Esophagus

Kidney

Testis

Notocord

Spinal cord

UPTURNED SPINE
The spinal column bends up to support the upper, or superior, lobe of the caudal fin (the tail).

TOP-POWERFUL TAIL
Since its upper lobe is larger than its lower one, the tail's thrashing movements don't just drive the shark forward – they also push its head down. This nosedive is countered by the fish's wedge-shaped head and its pectoral fins, which act like hydrofoils to lift the front end.

Second dorsal fin

Centrum (body) of vertebra

Rectal gland

RAYS FOR THE TAIL
The lower or inferior lobe of the tail is braced by long lower extensions of the vertebrae, called hemal rays.

Anal fin

Pelvic fin

Blood vessels to fin

SPERM JOURNEY
Sperm made in the testes pass along the Wolffian duct on the way to being stored and then expelled during mating.

ROTATING CLASPERS
The male shark has tube-shaped claspers developed from parts of his pelvic fin. During mating, he swivels these forward and inserts them into the female's cloaca (reproductive opening).

SANDPAPER SKIN
Notoriously rough and tough, sharkskin is covered with placoid scales, like tiny teeth all pointing backward.

PECTORAL FIN
The shark's propulsive power comes mainly from its tail. Its other fins are inflexible and it cannot "row" itself along with them, as can many bony fish.

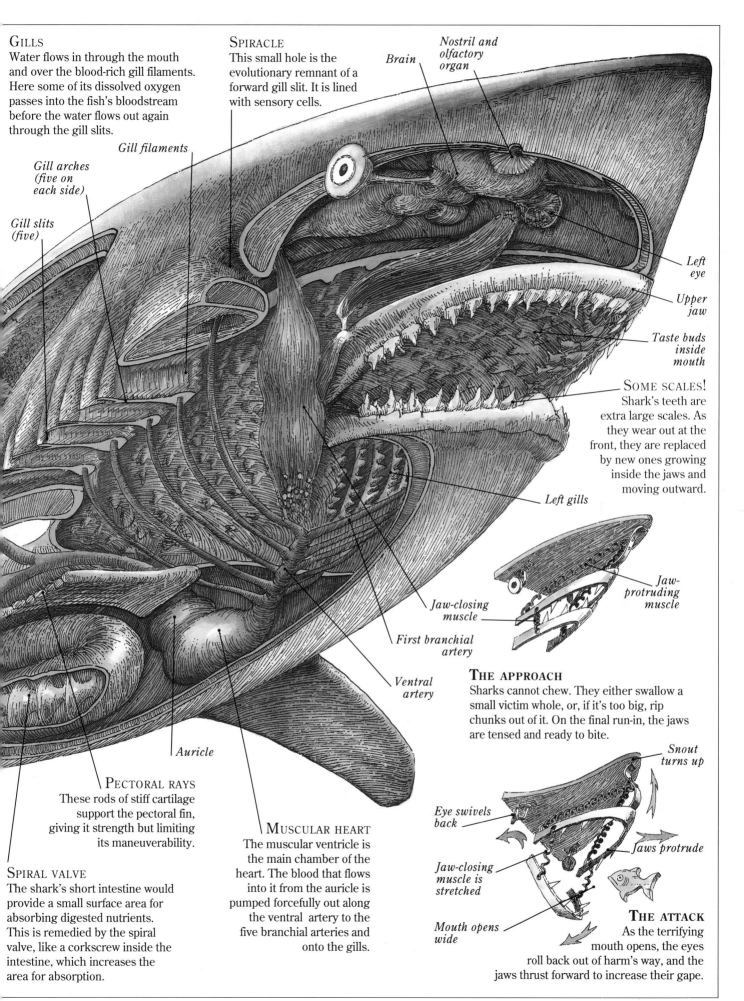

GILLS
Water flows in through the mouth and over the blood-rich gill filaments. Here some of its dissolved oxygen passes into the fish's bloodstream before the water flows out again through the gill slits.

Gill filaments

*Gill arches
(five on
each side)*

*Gill slits
(five)*

SPIRACLE
This small hole is the evolutionary remnant of a forward gill slit. It is lined with sensory cells.

Brain

*Nostril and
olfactory
organ*

*Left
eye*

*Upper
jaw*

*Taste buds
inside
mouth*

SOME SCALES!
Shark's teeth are extra large scales. As they wear out at the front, they are replaced by new ones growing inside the jaws and moving outward.

Left gills

*Jaw-
protruding
muscle*

THE APPROACH
Sharks cannot chew. They either swallow a small victim whole, or, if it's too big, rip chunks out of it. On the final run-in, the jaws are tensed and ready to bite.

*Jaw-closing
muscle*

*First branchial
artery*

*Ventral
artery*

*Snout
turns up*

*Eye swivels
back*

Jaws protrude

*Jaw-closing
muscle is
stretched*

*Mouth opens
wide*

THE ATTACK
As the terrifying mouth opens, the eyes roll back out of harm's way, and the jaws thrust forward to increase their gape.

Auricle

PECTORAL RAYS
These rods of stiff cartilage support the pectoral fin, giving it strength but limiting its maneuverability.

MUSCULAR HEART
The muscular ventricle is the main chamber of the heart. The blood that flows into it from the auricle is pumped forcefully out along the ventral artery to the five branchial arteries and onto the gills.

SPIRAL VALVE
The shark's short intestine would provide a small surface area for absorbing digested nutrients. This is remedied by the spiral valve, like a corkscrew inside the intestine, which increases the area for absorption.

33

COMMON STARFISH

WITHOUT HEAD OR TAIL, left side or right side, the wandering starfish is a central disk with five arms. (Or are they legs?) This shallow-water predator is an echinoderm, a member of an exclusively sea dwelling group, 6,000 species strong. Echinoderms have radial symmetry, that is, a circular body plan, based on several interconnected networks of muscle-powered tubes. Each network involves hundreds of tube-feet, and is used for moving and feeding.

EXIT TOPSIDE
The starfish's anal opening lies roughly in the center of the upper surface, almost invisible among the skin accessories. Liquid wastes stored in the rectal sac are squirted out at intervals and carried away by water currents.

Anal opening

Upper hemal ring

SEA BREEDER
In each arm, two gonads open by small ducts onto the upper surface. These make eggs (or sperm) for reproduction, which the female (or male) starfish tosses into the sea, leaving fertilization to chance.

SKIN ACCESSORIES: 1
Besides the spines, many sense receptors are scattered across the starfish's skin. They detect touch, water currents, and chemicals floating in the seawater.

MADREPORITE
This sievelike plate is the entrance to the water vascular system that operates the tube-feet. The "water" in the system is very similar to seawater, with some organic substances such as proteins, as well as a few cells, floating in it.

Mouth

Stomach

Main nerve ring

Pyloric duct

SKIN ACCESSORIES: 2
Dotted over an echinoderm's surface are tiny pincerlike organs on movable stalks. These are pedicellariae, which grab and remove any small pest or irritating item on the skin.

Hemal vessel

Hemal ring (circular blood vessel)

GUT POUCHES
The central stomach is linked to two pyloric caeca in each arm. These digest and absorb food.

REPLACEMENT PARTS
Starfish can regrow up to four new arms to replace lost ones, so long as the creature's central disk stays mostly intact. In olden times, fishermen cut up starfish that were damaging oyster beds. The fishermen only made things worse, unaware that those cut in two regenerated into new starfishes.

UNDERWATER BREATHING

Thin-walled gill tufts containing body fluid project through the tough skin. They take in oxygen from the surrounding water; waste carbon dioxide passes in the opposite direction.

Gill tufts

ARM-TIP EYE

At the end of each arm, a few tube-feet have evolved into light-detectors. They form a simple eye, the optic cushion, that can sense patterns of light and dark – as when the shadow of a predator falls over the starfish.

Ossicle in undersurface of arm

CRYSTAL PLATES

Hard calcite crystals, ossicles, are embedded in the skin forming a protective, flexible, outer casing. In some starfish the ossicles have spikes and spines.

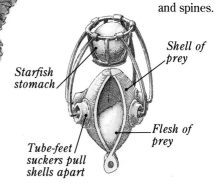

Shell of prey

Starfish stomach

Flesh of prey

Tube-feet suckers pull shells apart

SUCKED TO DEATH

A hungry starfish stands over a mussel, cockle, or clam. It clamps its tube-feet onto the victim's shell, and pulls steadily for about half an hour, using its tube-feet in relays …

BLOOD SYSTEM

The hemal tuft controls the composition of the starfish's blood, which oozes slowly through a system of hemal vessels into each arm. The vessels are linked by two hemal rings above the stomach, and one around the mouth.

Upper longitudinal muscle

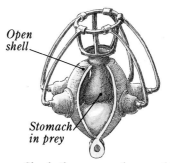

Open shell

Stomach in prey

… Slowly the prey weakens and its shell gapes slightly. The starfish turns its stomach inside out and pushes it through the gap, to digest the flesh within.

Ossicles between tube-feet

Radial water canal

Ossicle

Lower longitudinal muscle

BENDY ARM

The lower and upper strands of longitudinal muscle work in conjunction with the water system, so the starfish can twist and bend each arm on its own.

RESERVOIR BULB

As the tube-foot withdraws and shrinks, its water flows into the ampulla, an expandable bulb above it. This localizes pressure in the system.

MARCHING FEET

Muscles in the tube-feet walls can point them sideways, forward, and backward, making them all move the same way.

STICKY SOLE

The tubelike foot is tipped with mucous glands that make the sucker sticky, and give it a good grip.

THE TUBE-FEET

A starfish walks on dozens of tiny tube-feet, arranged in two rows under each arm. The feet are lengthened or pulled in by hydraulic pressure from a water-filled radial canal in each arm.

BANDED SNAIL

UNDER COVER OF NIGHT, the snail slides from its hiding place among the stones and heads for the vegetable patch. Its muscular "foot," which marks it as a member of the vast mollusc group, leaves behind a trail of silvery mucus glistening in the moonlight. The rest of the snail's extremely pliable body is wrapped inside a folded-over bag, the mantle, and housed inside a hard, spiraling shell.

WATER ECONOMY
The kidney produces concentrated wastes, since the moisture-loving snail cannot afford to waste water.

Waste tube to anus

SNAIL'S STOMACH
This expandable sac holds shaved-off food particles while the nutrients in them are absorbed through its wall.

Rectum

SNAIL'S PACE
Wavelike muscular contractions along the base of the foot propel the snail forward at around 40 inches per minute – that's .037 miles per hour.

CUSHION OF SLIME
Gastropodal mucus (better known as slime) helps the snail to grip the ground and slide along. It is formed mainly in tiny glands along the upper part of the foot.

Trailing edge of foot

Muscle strands

Heart

Seminal receptacle

Columnella

36

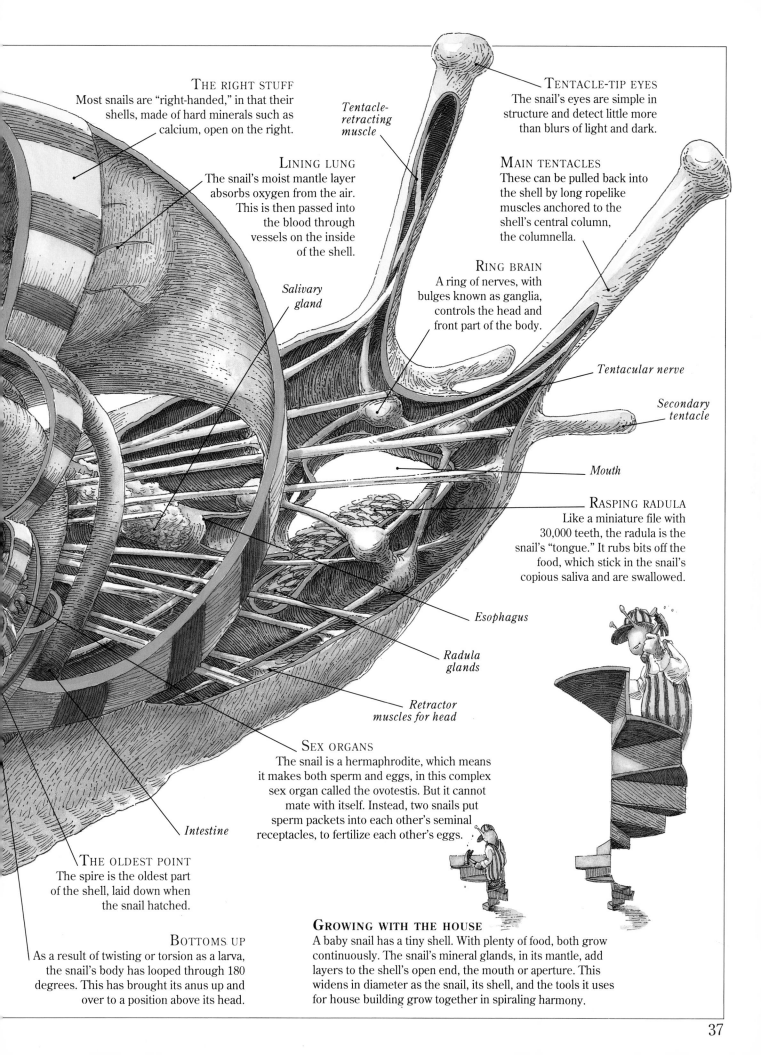

THE RIGHT STUFF
Most snails are "right-handed," in that their shells, made of hard minerals such as calcium, open on the right.

Tentacle-retracting muscle

TENTACLE-TIP EYES
The snail's eyes are simple in structure and detect little more than blurs of light and dark.

LINING LUNG
The snail's moist mantle layer absorbs oxygen from the air. This is then passed into the blood through vessels on the inside of the shell.

MAIN TENTACLES
These can be pulled back into the shell by long ropelike muscles anchored to the shell's central column, the columnella.

Salivary gland

RING BRAIN
A ring of nerves, with bulges known as ganglia, controls the head and front part of the body.

Tentacular nerve

Secondary tentacle

Mouth

RASPING RADULA
Like a miniature file with 30,000 teeth, the radula is the snail's "tongue." It rubs bits off the food, which stick in the snail's copious saliva and are swallowed.

Esophagus

Radula glands

Retractor muscles for head

SEX ORGANS
The snail is a hermaphrodite, which means it makes both sperm and eggs, in this complex sex organ called the ovotestis. But it cannot mate with itself. Instead, two snails put sperm packets into each other's seminal receptacles, to fertilize each other's eggs.

Intestine

THE OLDEST POINT
The spire is the oldest part of the shell, laid down when the snail hatched.

BOTTOMS UP
As a result of twisting or torsion as a larva, the snail's body has looped through 180 degrees. This has brought its anus up and over to a position above its head.

GROWING WITH THE HOUSE
A baby snail has a tiny shell. With plenty of food, both grow continuously. The snail's mineral glands, in its mantle, add layers to the shell's open end, the mouth or aperture. This widens in diameter as the snail, its shell, and the tools it uses for house building grow together in spiraling harmony.

BLUE-RINGED OCTOPUS

A STEALTHY AMBUSHER of crabs and prawns, the octopus is the most complex member of the mollusc family. Unlike its distant cousins, snails and clams, it has lost its hard, protective shell during millions of years of evolution. It relies instead on two large eyes, eight sensitive arm tips, and a well-developed brain to keep out of trouble. Its body core is also protected by a large fold of flesh, the mantle, which wraps around it like a monk's hood. Beneath the mantle, in the watery space known as the mantle cavity, lie the gills, blood vessels, and other delicate parts.

The blue-ringed octopus is one of the most dangerous animals in the sea. If threatened, it lashes out with its beaklike mouth and stabs a mixture of saliva and fast-acting nerve poison into the molester. Paralysis and death can follow in minutes.

Sphincter contracts

Sucker pushes against surface

SQUASHING DOWN...
Each sucker has two rings of muscle called sphincters. As these contract, they force water out of the sucker chamber.

Sucker chamber expands

Sphincter stays taut

... AND SUCKING ON
When other muscles pull the chamber up, water pressure from outside clamps the sucker to the surface.

Water pressure clamps sucker

Third right arm

Nerve to arm

Second right arm

WALKING ON ARMS
The octopus crawls delicately over the sea bed, feeling with its arms and gripping with their two rows of suckers. The extremely sensitive arm tips explore cracks and crannies for potential food.

First left arm

First right arm

Nerve

Artery

Main muscle mass

Nerve pathways

Lower sucker sphincter

DEADLY EMBRACE
When it comes upon a crab, the octopus grabs its victim in its suckered arms and cracks the shell with its beak.

BLUE FOR DANGER
If the blue-ringed octopus is threatened, dull patches on its body and arms suddenly glow with electric-blue hoops. If its enemy doesn't heed the warning, the animal strikes.

INSIDE AN ARM
Each arm has 10 sets of main muscles, controlled by an array of nerve networks and nourished by two major arteries.

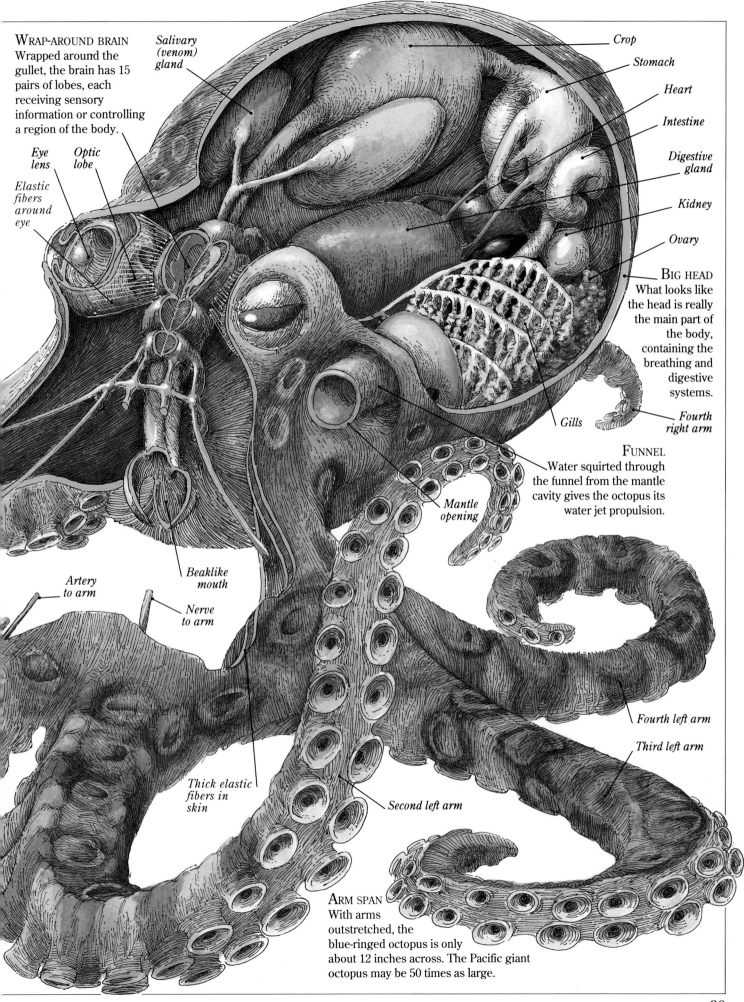

WRAP-AROUND BRAIN
Wrapped around the gullet, the brain has 15 pairs of lobes, each receiving sensory information or controlling a region of the body.

Salivary (venom) gland

Crop

Stomach

Heart

Intestine

Digestive gland

Kidney

Ovary

Eye lens

Optic lobe

Elastic fibers around eye

BIG HEAD
What looks like the head is really the main part of the body, containing the breathing and digestive systems.

Gills

Fourth right arm

FUNNEL
Water squirted through the funnel from the mantle cavity gives the octopus its water jet propulsion.

Mantle opening

Artery to arm

Nerve to arm

Beaklike mouth

Fourth left arm

Third left arm

Thick elastic fibers in skin

Second left arm

ARM SPAN
With arms outstretched, the blue-ringed octopus is only about 12 inches across. The Pacific giant octopus may be 50 times as large.

39

HONEY BEE

THE WORKER BEE shares her busy hive with 50,000 of her closest relatives – mostly other workers, who are her sisters. Her jobs are many and never-ending. She collects nectar and pollen from up to three miles away. Then she processes them into honey to be eaten by the growing grubs in their waxen cells. She cleans and repairs the honeycombs, and defends her queen mother and the rest of the hive against bears, people, and other hungry beasts who brave the bees' poison stings.

VEINS
The wing membrane is supported by stiff, branching veins. The blood they supply nourishes the transparent, living membrane.

FOUR WINGS
Each pair of wings flaps as one, linked by a row of hooks on the rear wing that clip into a groove in the front one.

Honey stomach

TWIN STOMACHS
The honey stomach processes nectar into honey, which the bee regurgitates back at the hive. A small amount passes to the main stomach, just behind it, to nourish the bee's own body.

Overlapping plates of exoskeleton

FIVE HEARTS
The five muscular bulges in the bee's main blood vessel squeeze rhythmically from back to front, to circulate blood around the body.

Malpighian organs (see p.42)

RECTUM
At the end of the digestive tract, the muscular rectum shapes, stores, and finally expels droppings.

SCENT GLAND
The Nasanov gland releases smell chemicals called pheromones. Each hive has its own unique scent. The worker and her sisters spray this over their hive, flowers, and territory to warn off rival swarms.

KAMIKAZE STING
The barbed sting lodges deep in the thick skin of a person. When the bee tries to fly away, its whole rear end is ripped off. The insect flies away and dies, leaving its sting and poison sac still pumping venom into its victim.

Air holes (see p.42)

Intestine

POLLEN BASKET
Back legs have extra-hairy second and third segments to hold sticky pollen grains.

Air tubes

Poison sac

Sting-extending muscles

40

COMPOUND EYE
This sensory mosaic detects the ultraviolet light reflected by the honey guidelines of petals. These lines lead the bee straight to the nectar.

Flight muscles

Air sac

Sucking muscles

Maxillary palp

Maxilla (tongue sheath)

Labial palp

Glossa

Main nerve

Salivary gland

Eye brush

Antenna brush

Pollen brush

Tarsal claws on leg tips

Antenna

JELLY GLAND
The hypopharyngeal gland makes "royal jelly," a high-protein baby food. Larvae fed on royal jelly for six to eight days become workers or drones, while those nourished on it until they are fully grown turn into queens.

Brain

PHARYNX
This powerful, muscular pump squeezes nectar up into the honey stomach.

Mandibles or jaws

MOUTHPARTS
The bee's complex mouth includes palps, which detect tastes and textures, and a long, hairy tongue, the glossa, with a deep groove. This laps nectar up into the pharynx.

THE CLICKBOX WINGBEAT

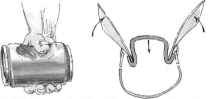

A bee's flight muscles beat its wings indirectly, by changing the thorax shape. One set pulls the upper thorax down, clicking the wings up. A squeezed metal can dimples in the same way.

Squeeze the can's base and the dimple pops out. The bee does this with another set of flight muscles, which snap the thorax back and jerk the wings down. The bee's "hum" is produced as it flaps its wings in this way, 250 times a second!

CLEAN BEE
Each front leg has three brushes. The hairy second segment sweeps dust off the bee's eyes. The bristly third segment scrapes pollen from flowers into the pollen basket. The circular cutout between them is an antenna-cleaning brush.

MOSQUITO

RIGHT AFTER MATING, the female mosquito goes off in search of a sleeping animal. A tiny prick in the skin, a few minutes sucking, and she flies into the night with a droplet of fresh blood. She has found the proteins to make her eggs – and left you with an itchy red spot.

BZZZZZZZZZZZZZZ
Being a member of the fly family, Diptera, the mosquito has one pair of wings. The female beats hers 400 to 500 times each minute.

Setae (sensitive hairs)

Fringes of scales

Egg sac

Rectum

Egg duct

AIR TUBES
Insects breathe through a network of tubes called tracheae, which open on the skin at tiny holes known as spiracles.

Pouch of gut

Spiracle

BLOOD MEAL
It takes the female mosquito no more than two minutes to suck up a stomachful (about a dram) of blood. She then spends three days hiding in a quiet spot, digesting her gory meal.

MALPIGHIAN ORGANS
Insects and other invertebrates have a system of tiny tubes threading their way around the abdomen. These collect and expel wastes from the internal organs.

LEG
Six muscles running down inside each tubular leg bend and straighten the various leg joints.

Setae at joint

LEG JOINTS
The hard body casing, or exoskeleton, is very thin at the joints. This allows the mosquito to bend its legs easily as it walks about in search of a good feeding spot.

Second tarsal section

First tarsal section

FOOT
The tiny foot is equipped with a pair of claws and a tuft of hairs (empodymium) for gripping the smoothest surfaces.

Fifth section of tarsus part of leg

Fourth tarsal section

Third tarsal section

MALARIAL MOSQUITOES
The female *Anopheles* mosquito spreads the deadly disease malaria. As she feeds on an infected person, she takes in the microscopic, disease-causing parasites in the blood. When she "bites" the next person, she injects some saliva and passes on the malaria parasites.

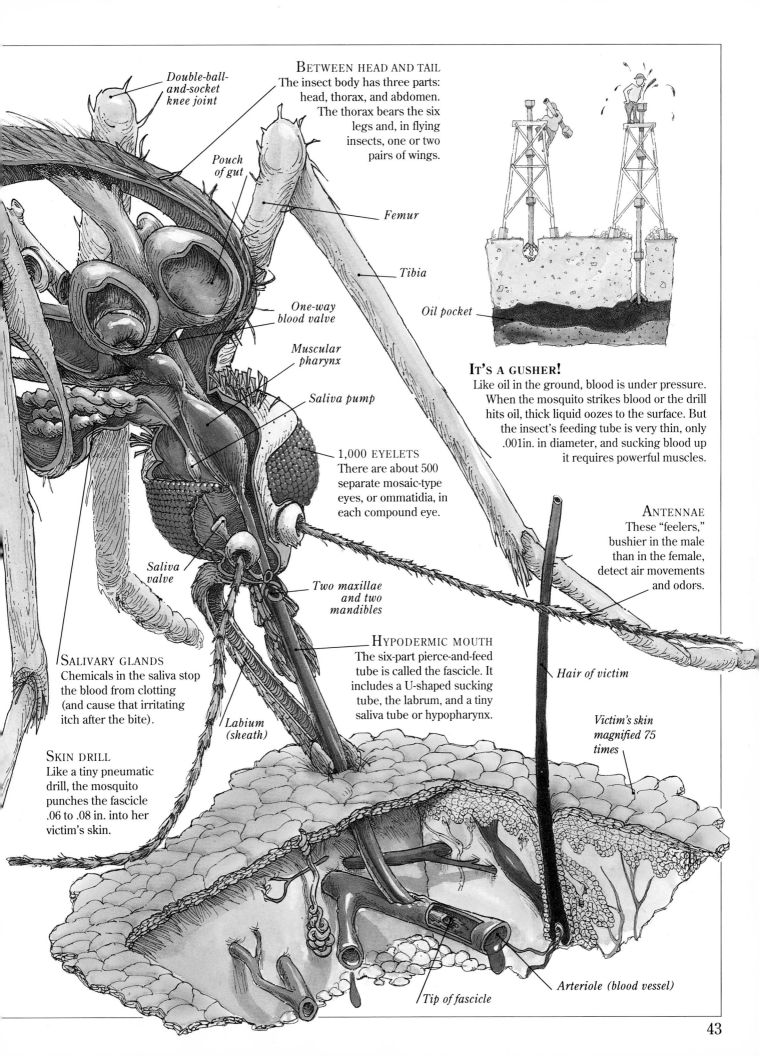

Double-ball-and-socket knee joint

BETWEEN HEAD AND TAIL
The insect body has three parts: head, thorax, and abdomen. The thorax bears the six legs and, in flying insects, one or two pairs of wings.

Pouch of gut

Femur

Tibia

One-way blood valve

Muscular pharynx

Saliva pump

1,000 EYELETS
There are about 500 separate mosaic-type eyes, or ommatidia, in each compound eye.

Saliva valve

Two maxillae and two mandibles

SALIVARY GLANDS
Chemicals in the saliva stop the blood from clotting (and cause that irritating itch after the bite).

HYPODERMIC MOUTH
The six-part pierce-and-feed tube is called the fascicle. It includes a U-shaped sucking tube, the labrum, and a tiny saliva tube or hypopharynx.

Labium (sheath)

SKIN DRILL
Like a tiny pneumatic drill, the mosquito punches the fascicle .06 to .08 in. into her victim's skin.

Oil pocket

IT'S A GUSHER!
Like oil in the ground, blood is under pressure. When the mosquito strikes blood or the drill hits oil, thick liquid oozes to the surface. But the insect's feeding tube is very thin, only .001in. in diameter, and sucking blood up it requires powerful muscles.

ANTENNAE
These "feelers," bushier in the male than in the female, detect air movements and odors.

Hair of victim

Victim's skin magnified 75 times

Arteriole (blood vessel)

Tip of fascicle

SPIDER

WITH EIGHT HAIRY LEGS moving like frantic fingers, the scuttling spider sends a chill of fear through most people. Yet only a handful of the 30,000 species of spider have all the deadly attributes it takes to harm a person – strong venom, jaws that can pierce human skin, and a tendency to attack rather than flee. The rest pose little threat to our safety. In fact, they help to keep down real pests such as disease-spreading flies. Spiders belong to a group of hunters called arachnids, and most of them feed on their six-legged relatives the insects. They all have venom glands for subduing their prey, and most spiders use threads of homemade silk to snare or truss up their tiny victims.

EIGHT EYES
Some spiders have two eyes on top of the head, one on each side, and a row of four across the forehead.

Palp

Brain

Venom glands

Venom duct in fang

Esophagus

Mouth

Muscles of stomach

Sucking stomach

Coxa

FLESH SOUP
After poisoning its meal, the spider pours digestive juices onto it and crunches up the softer bits. Then it sucks up the resulting thick soup with the powerful muscles of its sucking stomach, just as your mouth sucks a thick milkshake up a straw.

Branches of gut

Trochanter

SLUNG LOW FOR STABILITY
The spider's eight long, curving legs keep its abdomen close to the ground. This gives the animal a low center of gravity, which stops it from tipping over. A similar design, stable at high speeds, is found in racing cars and dragsters. Stability is achieved by the low ground clearance for the body, the long wheelbase from the front axles to the rear ones, and wide track between the outermost wheels on each side.

Joints in exoskeleton

Tarsal claws

GRIPPING FEET
The spider builds and repairs its web with the tarsal claws and tufted hairs on each foot. The middle claw and the hairs grip the silk like thumb and fingers as the spider clambers around its sticky trap.

LEG-SPAN
The largest spiders, such as *Lasidora* from South America, measure 12 in. from tarsal claw to tarsal claw and weigh over three ounces.

OPEN ARTERY
The spider's blood system is "open,"
meaning that its blood simply pours
out of the arteries, and sloshes
among the body tissues.

Femur

*Main
artery*

Patella

EIGHT KNEES
Spiders have eight legs, two more than
insects. Each leg has seven main parts: coxa,
trochanter, femur, patella, tibia, metatarsus,
and tarsus. This is one part more than an
insect leg, which has no patella, or "knee."

Tibia

Tarsus

Metatarsus

THROBBING HEART
The slow throb visible in the abdomen
of a large spider is caused by
the gentle pumping action
of its heart.

*Malpighian
tubule
(see p.42)*

(see p.42)

DIVERTICULAE
These tiny, dead-end tubes
form a network that carries
digested nutrients
throughout the body.

CLOACA
A storage sac for liquid
wastes, the cloaca's muscles
contract at intervals to pass
the wastes out of the body
through the anus.

Ovary

Egg duct

GLANDS
Aggregate gland makes sticky
drops for sticky web threads

Anus

SPINNERETS
These flexible organs, which
look like minute rubber gloves,
spin the silk into
multistranded bundles.

BREEDING
Eggs form in the female's two
ovaries. When mating, the male
spider fertilizes the eggs by
placing his sperm into the egg
duct in the base of her abdomen.

*Cylindrical gland
makes silk for
egg*

*Ampullate gland
makes non-sticky
web threads*

BOOK LUNG
Spiders have
two breathing
systems. One uses
tubes called tracheae,
as in insects. The other
is the book lung, a stack
of tissues like the pages
of a book, richly supplied
with blood, which absorb
oxygen from the air pocket
around them.

Leg muscles

A SELECTION OF SILKS
Most spiders have several types of silk
glands, each making thread for a different
purpose: web-building, tying up dinners,
and wrapping up their freshly laid eggs in a
protective nursery cocoon.

HARD AS SILK
The finest silk threads are
only 0.00003 mm (about one-
millionth of an inch) in diameter,
and the thickest are a mere
0.00015 mm across. Yet each silk
strand is three times as strong as
a steel wire of the same diameter.

45

SCORPION

LIKE ITS FELLOW eight-legged arachnid, the spider, the scorpion has a two-part body: the cephalothorax (front section) contains the head and legs, the abdomen behind contains the infamous venomous sting. Although scorpions are predators, they are more likely to use their poison in self-defense rather than attack. They may also use their powerful forearms, pedipalps, to seize and dismember prey.

INTERIOR OF THE POSTERIOR
The tail itself has five segments, plus the sting as the sixth. The main tail contains the posterior intestine, aorta blood vessel, and nerve ganglia (nerve trunk).

4 Femur

5 Tibia

3 Prefemur

56 LEG SEGMENTS
Each scorpion leg has seven segments, here numbered 1-7 for easy identification. The first pair of legs are usually the shortest, and the fourth (rearmost) pair the longest.

6 Basitarsus

7 Tarsus

End of intestine

Anus

Fourth tail segment

BOOK LUNGS
Each of the four pairs of book lungs is in its own chamber. This opens to the air below through a small aperture called, as in insects, a spiracle (see p.42). There are about 150 lamellae, or "pages," in each book lung for absorbing oxygen.

ARCHED ENEMY
The sting, officially known as the telson, is almost full of venom gland. Few scorpions have a sting which is deadly to humans, but the poison can cause great pain.

HUGE HEART
The heart is simply a pulsating enlargement of the main blood vessel, the dorsal artery.

Ventral nerve cord

2 Trochanter

1 Coxa

Main nerve to leg

Leg-moving muscles

PECTINES
This pair of feathery structures, unique to scorpions, have probably evolved from the forward set of book lungs. Their exact function is something of a mystery. They are probably sense organs, detecting vibrations in, and the smoothness of, the ground below.

46

AN UNFORTUNATE DESIGN

The scorpion's intestine finishes just under the sting. When the tail is held straight out behind the body, the creature can defecate as normal. However, if threatened, its anus is held precariously over its head.

ARMED AND ARMORED

The scorpion has one of the best armored exoskeletons in the business. The tough outer case thins at the joints to allow movement. However, many of the joints telescope into one another slightly, and can lock for greater strength. The exoskeleton also prevents water loss, and is a firm base for muscle anchorage.

Flexible tail weapon

Highly protective body plates

See-through visor

Ridged claws for grip and cutting power

Menacing claws on jointed arms

Jointed leg armor

CARAPACE

This hard head shield covers and protects the upper side of the cephalothorax.

TWO SETS OF EYES

There are two sets of scorpion eyes. These two median eyes can make out images and movements. The much smaller lateral eyes detect the overall level of light.

PINCER MOVEMENTS

A scorpion has more than 150 pairs of muscles which move its exoskeleton (compared to more than 300 pairs in a human). The muscles in the pedipalp make it wave menacingly at an enemy.

PINCER PARTS

The pedipalps are constructed from the same basic segments as the legs (see opposite). This large end part is the tibia.

Tarsus of pedipalp

Patella of pedipalp

Coxa and trochanter of pedipalp

Esophagus

Brain

Femur of pedipalp

MAIN MOUTHPARTS

The pincerlike chelicerae are similar to the much larger pedipalps, but only have three segments each. They are moved by five muscles within them, and another 13 muscles extending into the main body. They tear up food.

POOR PREY

Most scorpions are active at night. They use their pedipalps to grab insects, spiders, and other arthropods (joint-legged creatures), including other scorpions.

A SENSORY CARPET

The pedipalps, chelicerae, and many other parts of the scorpion's body are covered with tiny hairs (bristles or setae). These detect vibrations, and in some cases chemical tastes or smells.

47

INDEX

ACKNOWLEDGMENTS

The illustrator and author would like to thank:
• James Kirkwood, Head Veterinary Scientist at Regent's Park Zoo, London
• The staff of the Zoology Library of the Natural History Museum, London
• The staff of the Wolfson Library of the Zoological Society, London
• The Cob Breeding Company, Chelmsford, Essex, and Sovereign Chicken Ltd, Eye, Suffolk
• The countless anatomists over the centuries, whose endless pulling, poking and prodding around inside every creature under the sun, has provided the raw material for this book

Dorling Kindersley would like to thank:
• Sophie Mitchell, Colin Walton, Manisha Patel, and Meriel Yates for editorial and design guidance